Saint
THOMAS
BECKET

CHRISTOPHER HARPER-BILL

CATHEDRAL GIFTS LTD

THOMAS BECKET, the best known of all English saints, although a Londoner by birth, will always be associated primarily with the Cathedral church of Canterbury. He served as archdeacon of the diocese before he became archbishop. He staunchly defended the privileges of his office and his church, and in 1170 he returned to England to face martyrdom in the Cathedral for them. Within a few years the cult of the murdered archbishop raised Canterbury to the status of a major centre of western European pilgrimage, while his example was an inspiration to all.

The story of the relationship between Archbishop Thomas Becket and his earthly lord, King Henry II, has a perennial fascination because it involved the clash of two

St. Thomas, vested for Mass, in a modern copy of an early 13th-century representation. This stained-glass panel comes from the north aisle of the Trinity Chapel; the numerous representations of St Thomas in the Cathedral were destroyed in the time of Henry VIII and in the Puritan Commonwealth.

The site of St Thomas's martyrdom, in the north-west transept of Canterbury Cathedral. The altar, known as the 'altar of the sword's point', with the bronze sculpture representing the cross and two swords above it, was given this new form in 1986.

powerful personalities. Their conflict has, however, more fundamental significance. It was one particularly dramatic episode in the long struggle, lasting from the late eleventh to the early fourteenth century, between a universal church under papal leadership and the feudal monarchies which were to develop into the nation-states of Europe. These rulers had at their disposal not only brute force but an increasingly sophisticated bureaucratic machinery, and the career of Thomas Becket before his elevation to the archbishopric is itself an illustration of the growing professionalism of royal government in the twelfth century.

Born in London in 1118 of Norman parents, Thomas Becket was educated at Merton priory and at a city grammar school. His passport to fortune was entry into the household of Theobald, Archbishop of Canterbury from 1139 to 1161. Thereafter he studied both law and theology on the Continent, but he was no scholar, and merely did enough to make his way as a top administrator. He was appointed archdeacon of Canterbury in 1154, and early next year the Archbishop commended him to the newly crowned young King Henry as his chancellor.

Becket turned this position of head of the royal writing-office into something new. He was no mere senior secretary, but became the formulator and executor of governmental policy. He proved himself a staunch ad-

vocate of monarchical control over the Church, rejecting papal interference. He planned a great, if ultimately abortive, expedition in 1159 to vindicate Henry II's claim to Toulouse. The magnificence of his embassy to the French king was widely remarked. He was a worthy and proud servant of one of the most powerful rulers of the western world. His celibacy and continence were hardly any indication of the dramatic change to come.

In May 1162 Henry obtained the appointment of Becket to the vacant archbishopric of Canterbury, intimidating monks and bishops into acceptance. Thomas desperately attempted to dissuade the king, realising that Henry's vision of close cooperation was a mirage. Once he sat in the chair of St Augustine his loyalties must lie not primarily with the King, but with God, the universal Church and his own see. His change of heart and mind was signalled by his resignation, to Henry's fury, of the chancellorship.

The conflict which developed over the next few years can be understood only in the context of the papal reform movement initiated in the late eleventh century, and associated primarily with Pope Gregory VII (1073-85). This reform was not confined to the Church in the narrow sense, but affected the whole Christian community, for the pope had decided that the root cause of all evils within society was lay domination of the clergy at all levels, but

most especially the tyranny exercised over the Church by kings. The Church must have freedom to fulfil its divine mission. Secular monarchs, who had for centuries enjoyed the status of God's deputies on earth, were suddenly demoted to being mere agents of papal and priestly authority. A king was inferior to any minister of the church, for priests had to answer to God even for the souls of princes. Western European rulers lost the intellec-

tual argument, but they did not, of course, abandon the struggle. They attempted to retain control of the Church through new administrative techniques, through intimidation and through their extensive patronage. In practice a balance of power emerged in the twelfth century in most kingdoms, but Becket determinedly adhered to the full programme of Gregory VII.

It was unfortunate for Becket, as a defender of ecclesiastical liberties, that the then pope, Alexander III (1159-81), was engaged in a difficult struggle against the German emperor Frederick Barbarossa (1152-90), who was seeking to subdue northern Italy and supported a rival pope. Alexander III spent much of the 1160s in exile, first at Sens and then at Benevento, and he simply dared not drive Henry II into the imperial camp by unreserved support for Becket.

Thomas's first months as Archbishop were charac-

Effigy of Henry II **Henry was buried in the abbey church of Fontevraud (Maine-et-Loire); beside him are his wife Eleanor of Aquitaine and his son Richard I. Fontevraud was a nunnery in the heartland of Henry's Continental dominions, and was one of his most favoured religious communities.**

5

Seal of Thomas Becket This was the Archbishop's personal seal; it may seem odd that it was made from an antique gem engraved with the figure of a Roman god or hero, but such antique gems enjoyed enormous prestige in the early Middle Ages.

Charter granted by Thomas Becket as Archbishop of Canterbury, one of the very few surviving charters from his time of office.

(right)
The 'Waterworks' plan, a double page from the Eadwine Psalter showing the plumbing system installed by Prior Wibert (1152-67). It is a unique surviving image of Canterbury Cathedral as it was in Becket's time, before the fire of 1174 that destroyed its east end. Becket's own palace is not shown, but was situated to top right of the church on the plan.

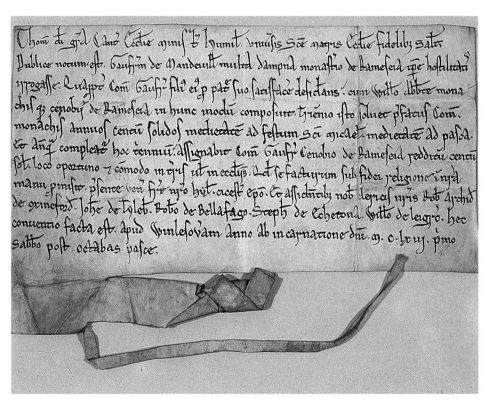

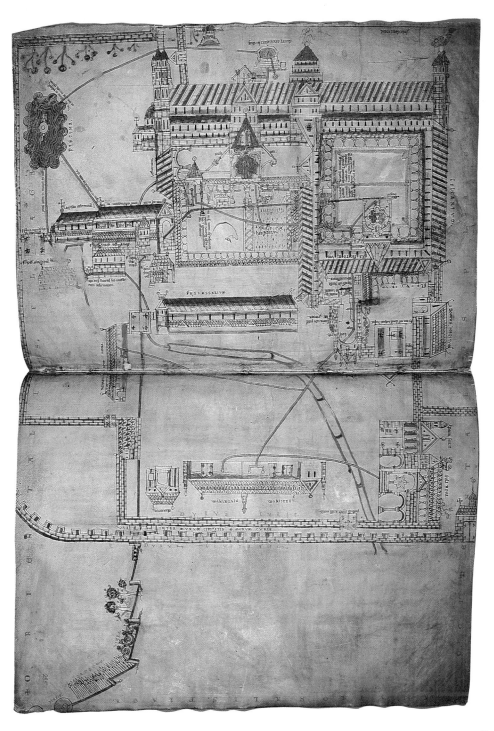

7

terized by a series of petty disputes, which indicated, however, that he meant to claim for the Church the entirety of that ambiguous borderland between royal and ecclesiastical jurisdictions. Matters came to a head in October 1163 when Henry II, as part of his great drive against all forms of criminality in England, proposed to the bishops that clergy convicted of misdemeanours and felonies in the Church courts should be handed over immediately to the secular arm for salutary and exemplary punishment. The King's stance is comprehensible, for clergy or 'clerks' included not only parish priests and monks, but married men who had received the first tonsure, perhaps as many in all as one in six of the adult male population. Becket, however, asserted that 'God does not judge twice for the same offence', and that degraded clerks should be answerable to the royal courts only for another crime subsequently committed. The canon law of the Church, which was only at this time beginning to be formulated, was ambiguous on this point. Becket, however, was determined to defend the complete autonomy of ecclesiastical jurisdiction. For him, the clergy should have no other king than Christ and should be subject to His law.

Faced by this resistance, Henry II broadened the issues at stake, and at a council at his palace of Clarendon in Wiltshire in January 1164 demanded that the bishops should accept sixteen 'constitutions' which set out the relationship between Church and Crown in England as it had been in the time of his grandfather Henry I (1100-35). The Constitutions of Clarendon not only restated the royal view on criminous clerks. They stipulated that cases about ecclesiastical patronage should be heard in the King's court, that no baron might be excommunicated nor might any bishop leave the realm nor any appeal go to Rome without royal consent, and that episcopal elections should in effect be controlled by the king. All this had been the situation in Henry I's time, but in the interim the English Church had achieved greater freedom, and not even the many royalist bishops felt that they could consent to such a scheme when set down in writing. Then, suddenly, Becket capitulated under pressure and agreed to Henry's demands. He soon repented bitterly and withdrew his consent, but this moment of weakness was disastrous, for it convinced most of the bishops that the former chancellor, whom they had never wanted as Archbishop, could not be relied upon.

Henry was now determined to break his former friend, whom he considered to have betrayed him unforgivably. Becket was cited to appear before the King's court as lord of Canterbury in a matter which was clearly feudal and temporal, rather than spiritual. He failed to respond and was hence guilty of contempt of court. With

Par lei roi enz crillez . | C umande par obedience . | Par sei ieunes e mecauint
D e thomas agrie a psuuitce . | E li uuire aucrnier timouce . | V eillet e afflictument
h onl deterie niel escharui . | C ilbo ne uolt estre acuintaux . | F ieblec enz le quoz ad fade
H e li tourestue li enchaui . | qz ait set cuiseilz e cunmand saire . | C rucher sen enz malade
H e la semuig ben gisune . | S i nun la uie enz perdue . | P ar force de obedience
T iene son enfant a la peine . | S a manere change e mue . | A mendra pluc cele abstinence

H e mangue fuel du pulment . | S i set amesuue nie suche . | C li aproscolle respunt
D unt serui su li ciuient . | D e fieblece mort geust . | E ile desturbe peche sunt
V iander arret sanz sauur . | qz ait deu ico par sauerru . | qz ail ne serrient legerement
V celle de nuit iure de iurs . | | P er force par cumun alcun
qz ait ico li enz de suffrir gref . | I a uie e saire rendu . | S il suussent audu pleint
T endre tu nurri e suef . | E nuit li roit dengleterre . | P ait serrient a tel parlement
T ant se mer en gnt destrece . | S aunr enz iure ne set ke sere . | S i ensemble eussetre parle
E il par tant tp sun cost blesce . | P putre uoiz de iur en iur . | T ost enterreient acorde
T rauailz kil ont auant duble . | S im repruuer e deshonur . | C mais li uoit ni asent pas
qz ait lestat de sun cont truble . | cq ur enz laidir e escharni . | k ensemble soient il e thomas
H e puer li cost sustenir . | C maudit un peste li . | i arceuesqz a co respunt
k eli quers ont en desir . | A la postolle enuoir a dure . | H e place a deu kisut le mund
P a ieunie adle quoa fade . | k e trop dure curreir celuie . | E pur nul mort suffrir en croiz
C ucher sen enz par tant malade . | k acord mult desire e uelt . | P e ni eusse la tierre uoit
P suen serui confessur . | k ele nest saire niur sen dorte . | k ar la pape par saul crire
k i nurlama par gnt redune . | qz essageit uienent e uint . | P urroit saut iugement seire
| k i alez e repairez sunt . |

In Pontigny, a Cistercian abbey near Auxerre in France, Thomas spent the first two years of his exile. He left the abbey in November 1166 after the King had threatened to confiscate all Cistercian property in England in retaliation. St Edmund of Abingdon, another canonised Archbishop of Canterbury (1233-40), is buried here. The building as it stands today is in the early Gothic style (late 12th century).

alexand papa

L i apostoillet bien entent
k e teu pes fature ni apent
d i assemblez ni fussent trois
l a pape e sil. e li rois
A u uoi mande ken nule guise
T ant froit unm serute iglise
l i message senuunt ataunt

O uant pes t...
e uire lemp...
l a pape de si...
k i muit pe...
l arceuesq. l...
G esq. en bu...
l a runge p...

8 th.

nur mise
nte iglise
sen part
la gaup
quoie
atte
rietarne

I enuiuic eli engres
ka tost destruiba cele pet
nuie ke puet deuenir
ke ne siet sa pes tenur
A u tirant henri mult pense
ke lateuesq; est tant d'eise
k'il sen uit ke nult lauue

(previous page)
Becket's story in the Getty Life: The parting of Becket and Pope Alexander III. One of the great legislators of the medieval Church, Alexander was himself in exile from Rome at Sens from 1162 to 1165. He supported Becket in principle, but was justifiably terrified that Henry II, if the Pope took up Becket's cause too energetically, would transfer his support to the Emperor Frederick I in his quarrel with the Pope, leaving Alexander in a very weak position.
British Library Loan MS 88; courtesy J. Paul Getty, KBE

(above)
Becket's story in the Getty Life: (on the left) St. Thomas excommunicating those accused of crimes and outrages. These sentences, delivered at Vézelay on Whit Sunday 1166, were directed not only against the King's agents but against the Bishop of Salisbury, a former supporter who had capitulated to strong royal pressure. Positions had hardened to a point where reconciliation seemed impossible. (On the right) The Council of Montmirail, January 1169, convened mainly to settle political differences between Henry II and Louis VII of France, but attended by papal legates. King Louis had protected Becket for over four years, but now became impatient with his apparent intransigence.
British Library Loan MS 88; courtesy J. Paul Getty, KBE

(facing page)
Vézelay in Burgundy, one of the foremost examples of French Romanesque architecture, was the centre of the cult of St Mary Magdalene, and was rebuilt between 1120 and 1150 on the proceeds of pilgrimage. Here in 1166 Becket excommunicated his adversaries.

Becket's story in the Getty Life: St Thomas leaves Montmirail, reproached by the two kings, Henry and Louis, and their followers, but the poor folk seek his blessing. He returned to Sens, where on Palm Sunday 1169 he excommunicated his great ecclesiastical rival, the Bishop of London.

British Library Loan MS 88; courtesy J. Paul Getty, KBE

St Thomas Becket, a stone relief set into the wall of the Cathedral of Sens. It is reputed to have been made originally for a private house in Sens, in the late 12th century.

Sens Cathedral, one of the earliest large churches to be completed in the new Gothic style, which originated in the area around Paris. Becket was in exile here from 1166-70, just at the time when the new Cathedral was being completed. It was no coincidence that the Sens master mason, William of Sens, commenced the new design of the eastern part of Canterbury Cathedral after the great fire of 1174.

this he was charged at the Council of Northampton in October 1164, when the King also accused him of financial dishonesty when he had been chancellor. Henry's behaviour at the council does him no credit. He harangued the bishops and cajoled the barons in order to obtain the verdict on which he was intent. Before it could be delivered, however, Becket stormed out of the Council. In disguise he took a circuitous route to the Channel coast, making ultimately for Sens and Pope Alexander, to whom he had already appealed.

The Archbishop was to remain in northern France for the next six years, first at the Cistercian abbey of Pontigny and then at Sens. There were constant diplomatic efforts to resolve the dispute, but whereas the issues at stake dominated Becket's and his circle's whole lives, for Henry II there were many other problems to be resolved in every province of his extensive empire, in none of which

Becket's story in the Getty Life: **The coronation of the young King Henry, eldest son of Henry II, on 14 June 1170, conducted by the Archbishop of York assisted by the Bishops of London and Salisbury. On the right the two Kings, father and son, are shown feasting. The heir to the French throne was often crowned during his father's lifetime, although this was a novelty in England.**
British Library Loan MS 88; courtesy J. Paul Getty, KBE

did the Archbishop of Canterbury find an imitator. The Pope, who returned to Italy in November 1165, supported Becket in principle, but seems to have despaired of his intransigence, which threatened to provoke the equally obstinate King into severing relations with the legitimate papacy just at the time when the independence of the Roman Church itself was under threat from a determined emperor.

Henry was uncharacteristically vindictive in his harassment of the Archbishop's kindred, friends and clerks, but Thomas responded in kind by excommunicating the King's main agents at Vézelay on Whit Sunday 1166. The bitterness of feeling is revealed by the exchange of vitriolic letters in that year between Becket and Gilbert Foliot, Bishop of London, a reforming prelate himself but one who believed that the welfare of the Church was best achieved by cooperation with the Crown. There were appeals and counter-appeals to the Pope, who despatched a succession of legates to resolve the dispute, but without any success. By 1169 a settlement seemed no nearer. At a conference at Montmirail in January Becket, by his refusal to accommodate, brought despair even to his protector, King Louis VII of France. In April he excommunicated Gilbert Foliot, his greatest ecclesiastical rival, who responded by claiming that London rather than Canterbury should be the archiepiscopal see. By the summer

21

(above)
Becket's story in the Getty Life: News of the young King's coronation
reaches Thomas (left) and the Pope (right). Becket was furious at this
violation of the traditional right of Canterbury to crown English kings.
This affront prompted him to return from exile, although none of the
fundamental issues at stake had been resolved.
British Library Loan MS 88; courtesy J. Paul Getty, KBE

(right)
Becket's story in the Getty Life: Thomas embarks for England on 1
December 1170. He is warned of treachery by Milo, chaplain of the
Count of Boulogne.
British Library Loan MS 88; courtesy J. Paul Getty, KBE

Viauð li produm le uout garnir · Milun sen uient bien tiant · Par une nef keð ariuee

A tant regarde e uoit uenir · Au passageur de Wihsant · E sur sa parole acertee

Q dun · quide keð eit desir · Sire uoleð ke uoirs uil tint · Uient eið bariner sunt

F ieit demander · e ficet uenir · De part mun seign le timt · Gar armee mil de krimp ·

S ire dub miller neeð pas sí · De Buloine · Armee gent · Guerre qut ariuerez

H e uient pas ficet demandeð · De la mer par mal uil atent · keð soieð tut tost detrenchez

C inz uut dit un mandement · S i nuuele tiuð seue · Par larceuesq Roger

O epart le timt eðe dolent · Del arceuesq en engletre · Empresteð de curuceð

H el uuð puit sanz lermes dire · Ceið dient ne uolent tere · C les eueðkes beð aueð

A turner sunt pur uuð ocire · keð disoient espessement · Suspenduz e escuminez

O e aduerðers grant asemblee · keð uendrat nouelemet · Que les cueiðeð bi reum

D e la la mer cumð iý armee · Q unt grant ioie euieð e hait · keð tumt uut sunt tut de krim

Quant ad le mandement oí · Q ait un de eult une part les tiaus · Renaud de Warenne ieit

T ut leð ebauð li respundi · ki dist retraet uuð chaitifs · Li uiðquens Geruede prest

O englecerre sui aler prec · S emble il iý lunger keð ir uifs · Candouf de Biue · ki ia

F ein sui tí p tut passer leð · Del cheualler une grant ríue · Li arceieiðt escuminia

D oit eðeke canterebire · De la uuð atent sanz dure · Of grant cunpaigne armee

C oz ore sun pastur deðir · ki pres sunt e apareillez · Tut ensemble afiancee

S era it ad eð io ni sui · De uuð ocire qui uendrent · A tendent sur la marine

ki du fiu arceuesq sui · Que eð la terre esmeue · bi iur e nuit guetter ne fine

tant regarde uð la bile · Cn uuð pmere uenue · He fereð plus tost ariuez

kð kune nef seariue · L ad ef sun ture ð iý metent · keð peiieð e deðruchez keð esbaie

k om demande que eð uenue · L arceuesq e suen tut retret · Dauant ure sa espasne · Co oriuur

Becket's story in the Getty Life: **Thomas lands at Sandwich. The king's vassals, under the Sheriff of Kent, line the shore in hostile attitudes. Becket was protected from them by his old enemy John of Oxford, who had masterminded the king's campaign against him, but now escorted him home.**
British Library Loan MS 88; courtesy J. Paul Getty, KBE

egales τ brokenfer

(above) *Thomas Becket's martyrdom* This is the earliest known pictorial representation of Becket's martyrdom, in British Library MS Cotton Bii, fol 341r, a manuscript dating to about 1180. It precedes the account of the saint's death by John of Salisbury, the greatest English scholar of the 12th century. In the picture, Reginald FitzUrse among the knights strikes the first blow; on the right the four murderers do penance at the tomb.

(right) This is a 15th-century version of the martyrdom (or rather a copy after the now faded original). Becket is shown encircled by his persecutors, in a composition recalling that of Christ flagellated or crowned with thorns.

(right) This representation of Becket's martyrdom comes from an English Psalter of about 1190-1200. The leader of the knights, Reginald FitzUrse, is distinguished by the heraldic device of a bear on his shield. The clerk whose arm was severed by a sword-stroke is Edward Grim, who would be one of Becket's biographers.

(below) This was one of many such reliquary caskets showing Becket's martyrdom made at Limoges in the 13th century; Limoges specialised in enamel work throughout the Middle Ages. This example is in the Burrell Collection in Glasgow; it may have belonged earlier to a Kentish town church, and in the 18th century was in the collection of Horace Walpole at Strawberry Hill. It portrays the martyrdom with the Hand of God stretching down through a cloud. On the lid is St Thomas in apotheosis between two angels.

Henry II feared an interdict on his lands, yet even now, at a meeting at Montmartre in October, the King refused to give the kiss of peace on which Becket insisted if there was to be reconciliation.

Becket's return to England was prompted by an event unrelated to the main conflict. On 14 June 1170 Henry, in order to secure the succession, had his eldest son, Henry, crowned by the Archbishop of York. This was a violation of the traditional right of the church of Canterbury, and marked a new phase in the rivalry of the two archbishops which had persisted since the Norman Conquest. Henry, once more afraid of ecclesiastical sanctions, met Thomas at Fréteval in July. He accepted Canterbury's position on the issue of the coronation, but there was no discussion of the Constitutions of Clarendon. Both parties felt that they had gained the day, which was hardly a solution. In fact, the Archbishop was now determined to return in order to protect the privileges of his own church. Landing at Sandwich on 1 December, he was met by the intransigent hostility of a gang of the King's men, but also by the adulation of the common people. His entry into Canterbury, as recounted by his biographers, had marked parallels with Christ's entry into Jerusalem on Palm Sunday.

Becket refused to absolve the Archbishop of York and the Bishops of London and Salisbury from the papal sentence of excommunication for their participation in the coro-

nation, and himself excommunicated those who had despoiled and still retained the archiepiscopal estates. It was these actions which prompted complaints to the King, still in Normandy. Henry had already been discussing with his councillors how the Archbishop might be restrained - house arrest was certainly envisaged - but his famous outburst, which provoked four prominent knights of his household to set out to kill him, was almost certainly unpremeditated. The words of the outburst are variously given, but most authoritatively were, 'what miserable drones and traitors have I nourished and prompted in my household, who let their lord be treated with such shameful contempt by a low-born clerk'. Equally surely, Thomas had not been courting martyrdom when he returned to England, but intended rather by a firm course of action to vindicate the rights of his see and of

King Henry II does penance at the tomb on 12 July 1174, as shown in 13th-century stained glass from the Trinity Chapel in Canterbury Cathedral. At the height of the crisis of his reign, with simultaneous rebellion in all his territories fostered by his external enemies, Henry came on pilgrimage to Canterbury. He was beaten by monks and bishops, made a large offering and lay in prayer all night. On the next day, his enemy the King of Scots was captured at Alnwick.
© *Sonia Halliday and Laura Lushington*

30

(left) *Trinity Chapel vaulting* showing the boss over the shrine of St Thomas from which the pulley to raise the wooden cover of the tomb chest was suspended.
© *Angelo Hornak*

The site of the shrine of Thomas Becket, in the Trinity Chapel, before its destruction under Henry VIII in 1538. Also an addition by William the Englishman to the work of William of Sens, the Trinity Chapel was ready to receive Becket's relics in 1220. The cover of the shrine could be raised on a pulley attached to the roof. The intricate marble pavement around the tomb still survives, as does much of the stained glass portraying a comprehensive sequence of the saint's miracles.
© *Angelo Hornak*

the Church against assaults both from the King and from petty predators. Yet when the four knights arrived at Canterbury on the evening of 29 December 1170 and confronted the Archbishop, and as the situation became increasingly violent, Thomas made no attempt to hide from them in the dark recesses of the Cathedral, but rather freely accepted death at their hands. When the terrified monks carried away his body, they found that he had worn a lice-ridden hair-shirt next to his skin, and had been daily whipped. We may be less inclined than contemporaries to take this as a mark of sanctity, but must at least admit that it indicates sincere penitence and stands in marked contrast to the outward pride of the Archbishop.

What Thomas achieved by his martyrdom remains a matter of debate. Certainly he reunited the English church, which had been rent asunder by his uncompromising stand on matters of principle. The bitter enemies of his latter years recognised the holiness of his end, and he became a model of episcopal resistance to governmental tyranny which was constantly cited to the eve of the Reformation. It is difficult to know what Henry II believed to be the outcome. The settlement which he reached with papal legates at Avranches in Normandy in May 1172 was a bargaining process rather than a royal capitulation. He agreed to abolish all evil customs which he had introduced, but since his entire case had been based on the

Stained glass in the Trinity Chapel: The four panels shown are from the fourth window of the north aisle - one of twelve magnificent such windows adorning the Trinity Chapel. At bottom right, St Thomas appears to King Louis VII of France in a dream. This King, who had protected Becket in exile, came to Canterbury on pilgrimage in 1179, presenting a valuable ruby (known as the 'regale of France') which was placed prominently on the shrine.
© *Sonia Halliday and Laura Lushington*

Shrine of St Alban, St Alban's Cathedral. The surviving shrine of St Alban was rebuilt in 1302-08; though different, it gives some idea of Becket's shrine as it must have been in its setting. Here a wooden gallery (in the background) was for custodians to watch over the shrine; there was also a watching chamber overlooking Becket's tomb.

situation in his grandfather's reign, he felt he had lost little. He did renounce jurisdiction over criminous clerks, but even here those forest offences which brought great profit to the Crown were excluded from this exemption. Henry and his sons appointed the same sort of men to bishoprics after 1172 as before. Yet the King was publicly humiliated when on 12 July 1174 he came on pilgrimage to Canterbury and was flogged by the monks before the tomb. His reward came swiftly, for the very next day the English sector of the great rebellion of 1173-74, which was the greatest crisis of his reign, collapsed, and William the Lion, King of the Scots, was captured at Alnwick. Still, the penance demonstrated that, however much practical control English kings might still exercise over the Church in the realm, there were limits to the measures of coercion which they could employ.

Sixteen months before Henry did penance, in February 1173, Thomas had been canonised by Pope Alexander III. The murder had shocked western Christendom, and some thought that the Pope had delayed unduly. At Canterbury the first miracle had occurred on the night of the martyrdom, and their multiplication eventually caused the hesitant monks in April 1171 to open the crypt, where the Archbishop had been buried, to

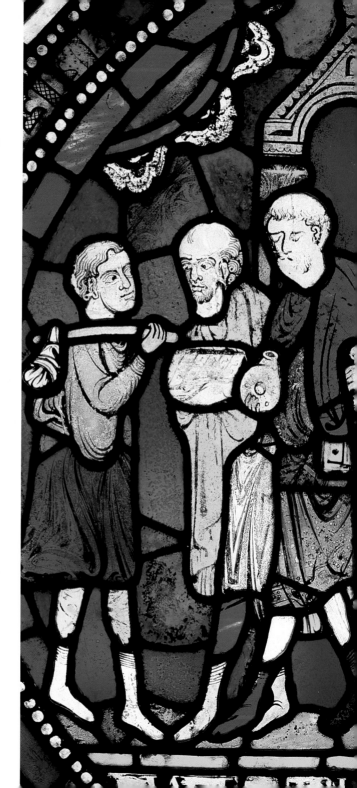

(left)

Stained glass in the Trinity Chapel: Pilgrims pray at the original low tomb in the eastern crypt, where St Thomas was buried from 1170 to 1220. The marble coffin was enclosed in a stone box with four port-holes, large enough for sick pilgrims to huddle as close as possible to the holy body.

© *Sonia Halliday and Laura Lushington*

(right)

Stained glass from the Trinity Chapel: In this detail, pilgrims to the shrine of St Thomas are shown bearing staffs, gourds, knapsacks and scrips or purses. All kinds of offering to the shrine were acceptable, including coils of wire. The pilgrims would carry away flasks of holy water or other more precious souvenirs.

© *Sonia Halliday and Laura Lushington*

pilgrims. The hostility of royal officials to the burgeoning cult lessened once Henry himself was absolved of complicity in the murder. Over 700 miracles are recorded in the decade after the assassination, and after the canonisation the beneficiaries included persons from the upper echelons of society and many from abroad, particularly from France. By 1200 the cult, and ampoules containing the martyr's diluted blood, had spread all over western Europe, from Iceland, where a saga about the saint was composed, to Spain

and Sicily. Canterbury rapidly became a great pilgrimage centre, the rival of Rome and Compostella, and it was almost a happy accident that a fire in 1174 necessitated the reconstruction of the entire east end of the cathedral. This created a spectacular setting for the proposed new shrine, although the body was not, in fact, translated from the crypt until 7 July 1220. The shrine was described by a Venetian visitor nearly three hundred years later:

Notwithstanding its great size, it is entirely covered with plates of pure gold. But the gold is scarcely visible beneath a profusion of gems, including sapphires, diamonds, rubies and emeralds. Everywhere that the

(previous page and above) *Chaucer's pilgrims.* In this recent painting by Eileen Thorne, pilgrims are shown winding their way along the road that leads to Canterbury. As then, so today, the story of St Thomas has a universal appeal to all classes of society, from the aristocracy to the lowest ranks of the afflicted.

eye turns something even more beautiful appears. The beauty of the materials is enhanced by the astonishing skill of human hands. Exquisite designs have been carved all over it and immense gems worked delicately into the patterns.

Far fewer miracles occurred at this magnificent tomb, however, than had at the simple sarcophagus in the crypt.

It is probable that the cult of St Thomas was declining in popularity even before Chaucer wrote *The Canterbury Tales* at the end of the fourteenth century. Shifts in popular piety caused it to be eclipsed by sites with relics of Christ himself or His mother. Yet hordes of pilgrims still came to the jubilee, held every fifty years after the translation of 1220, or great occasions such as the Black Prince's funeral of 1376. The only attacks and slurs came from a few isolated Lollard heretics, one of whom was executed as late as 1532 for insulting the martyr. When the end came, it was with remarkable suddenness. In 1536, when the Reformation was well under way in England, the government turned against the 'papist' archbishop who had resisted royal domination of the English church in an earlier age. In September 1538 the shrine was demolished, the bones dispersed and St Thomas's treasure carted off to Westminster. All liturgical commemoration was banned and a royal proclamation announced Becket to have been a rebel and a traitor. A spurious trial was held to 'prove' these allegations. The zeal with which Henry VIII and his servants attempted to eradicate all memory of St Thomas of Canterbury is, however, merely testimony to the example that he had provided for generations: that there is a law higher than the will of worldly princes, and that secular tyranny must, in God's name, be resisted even unto death.

View of the crypt
Canterbury Cathedral had the largest crypt in 12th-century England, essentially of the early 12th century, although the great columns sustaining the new choir above were added after the fire of 1174. It was in the crypt that St Thomas's body was first laid, until its translation to the Trinity Chapel in 1220.

© **Cathedral Gifts Ltd 1990**

Reprinted 1997

Written by Christopher Harper-Bill Designed and set in Palatino by Roger Davies, Green Street Press Produced by Scala Publications Ltd for Cathedral Gifts Ltd

Printed in Italy by Societa Editoriale Libraria per azioni

ISBN 0 906211 30 1